Alabama Spitfire

The Story of Harper Lee and *To Kill a Mockingbird*

WRITTEN BY Bethany Hegedus   ILLUSTRATED BY Erin McGuire

BALZER + BRAY
An Imprint of HarperCollins *Publishers*

Balzer + Bray is an imprint of HarperCollins Publishers.

Alabama Spitfire: The Story of Harper Lee and *To Kill a Mockingbird*
Text copyright © 2018 by Bethany Hegedus
Illustrations copyright © 2018 by Erin McGuire

ISBN 978-0-06-245670-0 (hardcover) — ISBN 978-0-06-303740-3 (pbk.)

The artist used Photoshop to create the digital illustrations for this book.
Typography by Dana Fritts
20 21 22 23 24   EP   11 10 9 8 7 6 5 4 3 2

❖

First Edition

To Katie Simmons, my spitfire sister,
and Kathi Appelt, my southern-sister-in-arms

–B.H.

For Susan Cohen

–E.M.

The red soil of Monroeville, Alabama, is as rocky as the state's past. But born in that same soil are the roots of the girl who grew up to write "the book of the twentieth century."

Nelle Harper Lee entered this world on April 28, 1926. From the get-go she was a spitfire.

Unlike her sisters, Alice and Louise, Nelle shunned what she called the "pink penitentiary" of girlhood. She embraced dungaree overalls, scampering up trees and rolling in tires like her brother, Edwin. Knee and elbow scrapes didn't bother her one bit.

In 1929, the Great Depression hit big cities hard. But in Monroeville, even during boom times, no one had much money. Neighbors were used to helping neighbors. But Nelle's hometown, even with its friendly folk, was still like the rest of the South.

White people and black people attended separate schools and drank from separate water fountains, and when it came to justice, separate was most definitely not equal.

Nelle's daddy, A.C., a lawyer, was a big believer in justice.
On hot, humid afternoons, instead of going to the movies,
Nelle watched him try cases at the courthouse.

In the evenings, Nelle would climb onto his lap to read the newspaper. Before she hit first grade, Nelle could read on her own.

Nelle loved words. She loved the sounds they made, how she could string them together to appease someone or to rile them up. Words had weight. Words held meaning.

CHUCKLED

SINGULAR

delicacy

establishment

peculiar

Bohemia

But when it came to schoolyard conflicts, Nelle preferred to use her fists.

It wasn't that Nelle was a bully—though she did have a temper—she just couldn't help but fight for what was fair. She always took up for the underdog. And no one was more of an underdog than Truman, a boy who came to visit his aunts for a spell and ended up living next door to Nelle.

Dressed in white linen suits, with a high-pitched voice, Tru was an easy target for bullies. Nelle became his friend and protector.

Nelle and Tru shared a love of books. Monroeville didn't have a public library, but as tight as money was, their families still made sure they both had books to read. Nelle's tree house became their secret hideout. From there, the friends could spy on the entire neighborhood.

One house in particular caught their curiosity. The shutters of the Bolewares' ramshackle house were always closed.

Nelle and Tru knew there was a story there. They watched. They whispered. They wondered.

Around this time, A.C. gifted Nelle and Tru with a black Underwood No. 5 typewriter. They took turns, one dictating stories based on their tree house spying and the other typing. Oh, the stories they wrote—"Old Mrs. Busybody" and "The Fire and the Flame." They were in hog heaven!

Until Tru's mother remarried and he moved to New York City.

Nelle missed Tru, but time marched on, even in sleepy southern towns. No girl stays a girl forever.

In college, Nelle didn't care about parties or fashion.
As editor of the school newspaper, she cared about
people, about words, about stories—both fact and fiction.

Nelle attended law school, like her father and her older sister Alice, but she didn't finish. The same girl who had typed in the tree house wasn't done telling stories. She made her way back to Monroeville to break the news that her dream was to be a writer.

A.C. didn't approve, but he knew he couldn't stop his headstrong daughter.

So in 1949, at the age of twenty-three, Nelle boarded a northbound train. Where was she headed? New York City, America's literary capital—and home to her old friend Tru!

The runt of Monroeville was now known as Truman Capote.
Like Nelle, he had never stopped writing. In fact, Nelle's pal
had made it big—he was a bestselling author! Nelle, once Tru's
protector, was taken under his wing. He introduced her to
all the important people. And in New York, there were many
important people.

Nelle settled into a small apartment in the Yorkville neighborhood, a long walk from the nearest subway. After a series of odd jobs, she began working the reservations counter at the British Overseas Airways Corporation.

Any chance she had, Nelle sat at her typewriter, the clicks and clacks of the keys mixing with the honks of the city traffic. She began with short stories. Writing, writing, writing. Revising, revising, revising.

Nelle worked day in and day out for seven years, but she didn't send out her stories. She didn't think her work was ready—yet. But Nelle was stubborn, and her Alabama spitfire streak would not let her give up.

Nelle's dedication didn't go unnoticed. Some of Tru's fancy friends saw how hard she worked on her writing, and on Christmas Day in 1956, Nelle found an envelope with her name on it pinned to their tree.

Dear Nelle,
You have one year off from your job to write whatever you please. Merry Christmas.

With the crash and clatter of the city all around her, Nelle left short stories behind. She began a novel. All those years of tree house spying served her well. Nelle started with what she knew best, writing about a small Alabama town inspired by her Monroeville roots.

The scents of perspiration and talcum powder, the memories of lazy Sunday afternoons, the hubbub of the town square, plus the drama of watching A.C. in the courtroom all got mixed together to make a story as satisfying as a serving of grits and gravy.

Nelle's first fifty pages landed her an agent. Then she wrote fifty more. And fifty more. Once her agent sold her book, she worked with her editor and rewrote it again. And again.

After three years and many titles, Nelle's book, *To Kill a Mockingbird*, was ready at last.

The world met the residents of Maycomb County on July 11, 1960.

Nelle, the girl who fought playground injustice, was at it again—publishing a book where a small town and its people struggled with what was wrong and what was right—and where skin color didn't automatically make one guilty.

Everyone in Alabama was talking about the book, too.

To Kill a Mockingbird flew off the shelves, making bestseller lists all over the country. It even won the Pulitzer Prize, the biggest literary award in the United States!

But Nelle's small-town story wasn't bound to be just a book—before long, it became an award-winning movie, too. Nelle, the Alabama spitfire, was famous.

But Nelle didn't like the limelight. The feeling of success, Nelle said, "was like being hit over the head and knocked cold." Nelle found herself in a new fight—one for her privacy. How would she tackle this? Not with fists. Not with stories. But what?

With silence! Nelle shut out reporters, declining interviews and rarely making public appearances.

Even so, her book continued to sell. *To Kill a Mockingbird* caused readers—all readers—to imagine themselves as Scout, as Atticus, as Tom Robinson, to "climb into his skin and walk around in it." In doing so, Nelle's book sold over forty million copies.

So what became of Harper Lee, the tomboy turned author? Did she hide away in the big city, where she was one of many, or did she seek solace in her hometown, where she was simply Miss Nelle?

Nelle chose both. For over forty years, she hopped trains and lived part of the year amid skyscrapers . . .

and part of the year amid Alabama fishing holes.

She carved out a life of her own design.

The red, rocky soil of her youth welcomed Nelle home for good in her eighties. Reporters still clamored for interviews, but Nelle's steely spitfire streak held strong.

At the age of eighty-nine, the girl who grew up to be Harper Lee died. Nelle is buried in Monroeville, the town she made famous in fictional form.

And *To Kill a Mockingbird* continues to do the speaking and fighting for her.

AUTHOR'S NOTE

For many, including me, there is no book more beloved than Harper Lee's *To Kill a Mockingbird*. It is taught, with chapters being excerpted, as early as fourth grade in schools all over the country. In Mr. Dikeman's fifth-grade class, I read the title scene, where Atticus encounters the rabid dog. I was hooked. That summer I read the book cover to cover, and did so once a year for over twenty years.

In surveys, *To Kill a Mockingbird* is listed after only the Bible as America's favorite book. Though beloved the world over, not much is known about its author, Nelle Harper Lee, who hadn't given a sit-down interview since 1964, just four years after its publication.

I began this book before the death of Harper Lee. As a writer, knowing how strongly my childhood shaped me, I started rooting around in Nelle's. Her early life in Monroeville, Alabama, had a major impact on her work and was where the story seeds for *To Kill a Mockingbird* got planted. In fact, the book spans three years—1932 to 1935—when Nelle, and the fictional Scout, grew from six to nine years old. And of course, there is Nelle's friendship with Truman Capote, who said in interviews that Scout, Jem, and Dill's attempts to get Boo Radley to make an appearance are "quite literal and true" and are based on their fascination with the Bolewares' son.

From 1949 to 1960, as a young writer in New York, Nelle worked tirelessly at her craft. As a reward for her diligence, Nelle's good friends Michael and Joy Brown funded her year of writing and helped her get her work seen by an agent, Maurice Crain. Crain liked her short stories but encouraged Nelle to write a novel. Crain sold Nelle's work in progress to publisher J. B. Lippincott, with an advance of a few thousand dollars. With her editor, Therese "Tay" von Hohoff, Nelle revised the novel that would become *To Kill a Mockingbird*. Nelle dropped her first name and published under the name Harper Lee. She didn't want her first and last names to run together, with Nelle Lee pronounced as "Nellie."

A few weeks after publication in July 1960, *To Kill a Mockingbird* was a top ten bestseller in both the *New York Times* and the *Chicago Tribune*. At a time when racial injustice garnered the national news spotlight, the book became a phenomenon. The same year the book was published, students in Greensboro, North Carolina, staged a sit-in at a segregated Woolworth's lunch counter and the Student Nonviolent Coordinating Committee (SNCC) was formed. Nelle's book may have been set in the Great Depression, but it also spoke to what was happening in the country in the civil rights era, when it was published.

In 1961, the novel won the Pulitzer Prize for fiction. In 1962, the film adaptation won three Academy Awards—Best Writing for Horton Foote's adapted screenplay, Best Actor for Gregory Peck's portrayal of Atticus Finch, and Best Art Direction. These awards secured both the book and the movie adaptation a place in history. The amount of interview requests and fan mail Nelle received increased. And in every interview, Nelle was asked about her "next" book. In one interview, she answered: "Yes, and it goes slowly, ever so slowly." But as time went on and another book did not appear, Nelle became more and more of a recluse. Her answer changed to variations of "I've said all I have to say."

When Nelle was eighty-eight, a novel she had written in the 1950s was discovered and released. *Go Set a Watchman* caused fans old and young to flock to bookstores and order copies online, creating another media frenzy. Nelle died seven months after *Go Set a Watchman*'s release. Amid all the hoopla, Nelle stayed silent. She continued to let both stories speak directly to the readers.

SELECTED BIBLIOGRAPHY

Cep, Casey N. "Mystery in Monroeville." *New Yorker*. February 20, 2015. www.newyorker.com/books/page-turner/mystery-monroeville-harper-lee.

Flood, Alison. "Harper Lee Breaks Silence—Just—for Mockingbird Anniversary." *Guardian*. June 28, 2010. www.theguardian.com/books/2010/jun/28/harper-lee-to-kill-a-mockingbird.

Langer, Emily. "Alice Lee, Sister of 'To Kill a Mockingbird' Author Harper Lee, Dies at 103." *Washington Post*. November 18, 2014. www.washingtonpost.com/entertainment/books/alice-lee-sister-of-to-kill-a-mockingbird-author-harper-lee-dies-at-103/2014/11/18/1d37b0c2-6f38-11e4-ad12-3734c461eab6_story.html.

Newquist, Roy, ed. "Harper Lee." *Counterpoint*. Chicago: Rand McNally, 1964.

Thomas, Louisa. "Who Helped Harper Lee with 'Mockingbird'?" *Newsweek*. July 30, 2010. www.newsweek.com/who-helped-harper-lee-mockingbird-74261.

Tooley, Mark D. "Harper Lee's Character 'Atticus Finch' Upheld the Family Legacy." *Christian Post*. December 15, 2014. www.christianpost.com/news/atticus-finch-in-a-skirt-131195/.

VIDEOS

"Harper Lee Alabama," www.youtube.com/watch?v=jRaQ6pMTe1Y.

"'To Kill a Mockingbird' Turns 50," *CBS Sunday Morning*, www.youtu.be/NHpuMF0iMx4.

"To Kill a Mockingbird: Successes and Myths," Alabama Department of Archives & History, www.youtu.be/F4hBiyGBORs.